Sarah Louise Arnold

Learning to Read

Suggestions to teachers of young children

Sarah Louise Arnold

Learning to Read

Suggestions to teachers of young children

ISBN/EAN: 9783337219116

Printed in Europe, USA, Canada, Australia, Japan

Cover: Foto ©Paul-Georg Meister /pixelio.de

More available books at **www.hansebooks.com**

SUGGESTIONS TO TEACHERS OF YOUNG CHILDREN

BY

SARAH LOUISE ARNOLD

SUPERVISOR OF SCHOOLS, BOSTON, MASS.; AUTHOR OF
"STEPPING STONES TO LITERATURE," "WAYMARKS," ETC.

SILVER, BURDETT AND COMPANY
NEW YORK ... BOSTON ... CHICAGO
1899

GREETING.

To Teachers of Little Children:

This little book is an outcome of schoolroom experience, and its "excuse for being" arises from an earnest desire to lend a hand to fellow-workers in a common cause. No sleight-of-hand or trick of the trade can serve as a patent and all-sufficient device in teaching reading. Hard work and ready wit, together with knowledge of child-life and love of teaching, — these must make the way to success. But a study of the experience of others may throw some light on the path of the young learner, — a path difficult enough at best in the early days. These hints and suggestions will fulfil their mission if they serve, even in slight degree, to answer the questions and solve the problems of the young teacher, whose privilege it is to lead her children into the Promised Land of Books. These pages are written in such hope, and go forth with cordial greeting to all whom they can serve.

SARAH LOUISE ARNOLD.

CONTENTS.

	PAGE
LETTER TO TEACHERS	3

CHAPTER
I.	HOW I LEARNED TO READ. *Hugh Miller*	7
II.	THE ART OF READING	13
III.	THE FIRST YEAR IN READING	31
IV.	LANGUAGE LESSONS, AS AN AID TO READING	67
V.	ILLUSTRATIVE LESSONS	77
	The Cow. *First Grade*	77
	The Oak. *First Grade*	81
	The Blacksmith. *Second Grade*	83
	The Rain. *Second Grade*	84
	Bird Life. *First Grade*	86
	The Builders. *Third Grade*	88
	Little Bell. *Third Grade*	90

LEARNING TO READ

CHAPTER I.

HOW I LEARNED TO READ.

From " My Schools and Schoolmasters." — HUGH MILLER.

I HAD been sent, previous to my father's death, to a dame's school, where I was taught to pronounce my letters to such effect in the old Scottish mode, that still, when I attempt spelling a word aloud, which is not often, — for I find the process a perilous one, — the *aa's*, and *ee's*, and *uh's*, and *rau's*, return upon me, and I have to translate them, with no little hesitation as I go along, into the more modish sounds. A knowledge of the letters themselves I had already acquired by studying the signposts of the place, — rare works of art, that excited my utmost admiration, with jugs, and glasses, and bottles, and ships, and loaves of bread upon them; all of which could, as the artist intended, be actually recognized. During my sixth year, I spelt my way, under the dame, through the Shorter Catechism, the Proverbs, and the New Testament, and then entered upon her highest form, as a member of the Bible Class; but all the while, the process of acquiring learning had been a dark one, which I slowly mastered, in humble confidence in the awful wisdom of the schoolmistress, not knowing whither it tended, — when at once my mind awoke to the meaning of that most delightful of all narratives, the story of Joseph. Was there ever such a discovery made before! I actually found out for myself, that the art of reading is the art of finding stories in books, and from that moment reading became one of the most delightful of my amusements.

I began by getting into a corner at the dismissal of the school, and there conning over to myself the new-found story of Joseph; nor did one perusal serve; the other Scripture stories followed, — in especial, the story of Samson and the Philistines, of David and Goliath, of the prophets Elijah and Elisha; and after that came the New Testament stories and parables. Assisted by my uncles, I began to collect a library in a box of birch-bark about nine inches square, which I found quite large enough to contain a great many immortal works, — " Jack the Giant-killer," and " Jack and the Bean-Stalk," and the " Yellow Dwarf," and " Blue Beard," and " Sinbad the Sailor," and " Beauty and the Beast," and " Aladdin and the Wonderful Lamp," with several other of resembling character.

Those intolerable nuisances, the useful-knowledge books, had not yet arisen, like tenebrious stars, on the educational horizon, to darken the world, and shed their blighting influence on the opening intellect of the " youthhood "; and so, from my rudimental books — books that made themselves truly such by their thorough assimilation with the rudimental mind — I passed on, without being conscious of break or line of division, to books on which the learned are content to write commentaries and dissertations, but which I found to be quite as nice children's books as any of the others. Old Homer wrote admirably for little folk, especially in the " Odyssey "; a copy of which, in the only true translation extant, — for, judging from its surpassing interest and the wrath of critics, such I hold that of Pope to be, — I found in the house of a neighbor. Next came the " Iliad "; not, however, in a complete copy, but represented by four of the six volumes of Bernard Lintot. With what power, and at how early an age, true genius impresses! I saw, even at this immature period, that no writer could cast a javelin with half the force of Homer. The missiles went whizzing athwart his pages; and I could see the momentary gleam of the steel, ere it buried itself deep in brass and bull-hide. I next succeeded in discovering for myself a child's book, of not less interest than even the " Iliad," which might, I was told, be read on Sabbaths,

HOW I LEARNED TO READ.

in a magnificent old edition of "Pilgrim's Progress," printed on coarse, whity-brown paper, and charged with numerous woodcuts, each of which occupied an entire page, that, on principles of economy, bore letterpress on the other side. And such delightful prints as these were! It must have been some such volume that sat for its portrait to Wordsworth, and which he so exquisitely describes as

> "Profuse in garniture of wooden cuts,
> Strange and uncouth; dire faces, figures dire,
> Sharp-kneed, sharp-elbowed, and lean-ankled, too,
> With long and ghastly shanks, — forms, which, once seen,
> Could never be forgotten."

In process of time, I had devoured, besides these genial works, "Robinson Crusoe," "Gulliver's Travels," "Ambrose on Angels," the judgment chapter in Howie's "Scotch Worthies," Byron's "Narrative," and the "Adventures of Philip Quarll," with a good many other adventures and voyages, real and fictitious, part of a very miscellaneous collection of books made by my father. It was a melancholy little library to which I had fallen heir. Most of the missing volumes had been with the master aboard the vessel when he perished. Of an early edition of Cook's "Voyages," all the volumes were now absent save the first; and a very tantalizing romance in four volumes, Mrs. Ratcliff's "Mysteries of Udolpho," was represented by only the earlier two. Small as the collection was it contained some rare books, — among the rest, a curious little volume entitled, "The Miracles of Nature and Art," to which we find Dr. Johnson referring in one of the dialogues chronicled by Boswell, as scarce even in his day, and which had been published, he said, some time in the seventeenth century by a bookseller whose shop hung perched on Old London Bridge, between sky and water. It contained, too, the only copy I ever saw of the "Memoirs of a Protestant condemned to the Galleys of France for his Religion," — a work interesting from the circumstance that, though it bore another name on its title-page, it had been translated from the French for a few guineas by poor Goldsmith in his days of obscure literary drudgery,

and exhibited the peculiar excellences of his style. The collection
boasted beside, of a very curious old book, illustrated by very uncouth
plates, that detailed the perils and sufferings of an English sailor who
had spent his best years of life as a slave in Morocco. It had its
volumes of sound theology, too, and of stiff controversy, — Flavel's
"Works," and Henry's "Commentary," and Hutchinson on the "Lesser
Prophets," and a very old treatise on the "Revelation," with the title-
page away, and blind Jameson's volume on the "Hierarchy," with first
editions of "Naphthali," "The Cloud of Witnesses," and "The Hind let
Loose." But with these solid authors I did not venture to grapple
until long after this time. Of the works of fact and incident which it
contained, those of the voyagers were my especial favorites. I perused
with avidity the voyages of Anson, Drake, Raleigh, Dampier, and
Captain Woods Rogers, and my mind became so filled with concep-
tions of what was to be seen and done in foreign parts, that I wished
myself big enough to be a sailor, that I might go and see coral islands
and burning mountains, and hunt wild beasts and fight battles.

Part I.

THE ART OF READING.

Part I.

CHAPTER II.

THE ART OF READING.[1]

BEFORE planning her lessons in reading, the teacher will do well to review her own experience in reading, or to scan the difficulties which she has encountered in teaching other classes. A brief analysis of her experiences, both as a pupil and as a teacher, will reveal distinct lines of achievement in learning to read. These are illustrated in any act of reading.

> "The old familiar sights of ours
> Took marvelous shapes. Strange domes and towers
> Rose up where sty and corncrib stood,
> Or garden wall, or belt of wood.
> The bridle post an old man sat,
> With loose-flung coat and high-cocked hat.
> The wellcurb had a Chinese roof,
> And even the tall sweep, high aloof,
> In its slant splendor seemed to tell
> Of Pisa's leaning miracle."

To read, — that is, to get the meaning of these lines, or, if one reads aloud, to get and to give the meaning. One who truly reads "Snow-Bound" learns to see the scenes which Whittier so beautifully describes; to see them as he saw them, with tender affection, and to interpret the deeper meaning of the lines of "homely toil and destiny obscure." Manifestly this involves much. On the surface, and first attracting the attention of the teacher, appears the obvious

[1] From "Reading: How to Teach It." — S. L. A.

necessity of knowing the words at sight. Familiarity with the forms of the words used is indispensable to reading. This involves knowing the sounds of the words, while the power to pronounce new words readily calls for knowledge of the laws of English pronunciation.

In the minds of too many teachers of little children, such mastery of word pronunciation is held as reading. But this is a grievous error, which leads to narrow and mechanical work, and obscures the high purpose of real reading. Reference to the definition of reading, and a study of the selection from "Snow-Bound," will show us the proper value of this achievement, and its relation to true reading. The words are the vehicle of thought, a means to an end. Their mastery is indispensable to reading, but the reader must compass, not the single word-speaking, but the meaning of the related words which express the author's thought. Knowledge of the meaning of the words used, and especially the meaning of the words as Whittier uses them, is necessary to a clear understanding of the poem. The reader who would understand the poem must know something of farm life — the sty and the corncrib, the garden wall, the wellcurb, the sweep, and the other accessories of the farm which Whittier names or describes. Plainly, too, his knowledge must extend further — to a Chinese roof, and Pisa's leaning miracle. To such knowledge, observation of common life must minister, coupled with the study of books and pictures. In other words, the reader interprets Whittier's "Snow-Bound" by virtue of his own experience, reënforced by the experience of others as written down in books, or pictured with brush or pen. To the formal word mastery, then, must be added study of the meaning of new words, or recalling such experience as explains the old. The content, as well as the form, of the word must be studied.

Added to such study, is the general training which gives us power to picture the unknown, interpreting a new scene through its relation to our old experience. The ready and trained imagination easily pictures the scene which the words conjure before the mind — makes real the homestead, snowbound and comfort filled. Reading may be so taught as to develop this power, which takes hold on things unseen. No careful teaching of reading omits this.

Here then are different phases of teaching reading: — mastery of the words, as to form and sound; explanation of the meaning of new words, through observation or reading; lessons which tend to develop power of imagination.

~~~~~~~~~~~~~~~~

The young child, who leaves his home and his play to enter upon the life of the schoolroom, finds a new world awaiting him, with manifold new experiences. Hitherto he has romped and rambled to his heart's content. All his friends and playmates have in turn been his teachers, albeit theirs has been an unconscious tuition. His lessons have been in the line of his desires, or suggested by his natural environment. Longfellow pictures the little Hiawatha in the arms of his first teacher, the loving old Nokomis —

> "At the door on Summer evenings
> Sat the little Hiawatha,
> Heard the whispering of the pine trees,
> Heard the lapping of the water —
> Sounds of music, words of wonder; —
> Saw the moon rise from the water,
> Rippling, rounding from the water,
> Saw the flecks and shadows on it,
> Whispered, 'What is that, Nokomis?'
> And the good Nokomis answered — "
> . . . .

The moon, the rainbow in the heaven, the Milky Way, the firefly, the owl and owlet, the beaver, the rabbit, the squirrel — these saluted the baby boy, and awakened his interest. "What is that?" he cried, with eager question. "And the good Nokomis answered." The little

Hiawatha "learned of every bird its language." He was taught, not by old Nokomis alone, but by bird and beast, flower and field.

So with every child who enters the schoolroom upon that fateful first Monday in September. He brings with him, not an empty head, but a mind stored with the memories of varied experiences. Just as the little Hiawatha gazed, pondered, questioned, learned — so this child has seen, has heard, has questioned, has thought, has acted. What he brings to school, who can tell? What has he seen and heard? What has he liked and desired? What has he questioned and learned? How little we know of this unwritten history! And yet it determines the net result of all our teaching. For nothing which we attempt to teach finds lodgment in the child mind unless it is linked with some past experience, and awakens actual interest. Much of our reiterated instruction falls upon deaf ears, fails utterly to awaken the dormant interest, because it is ill chosen. We must know something about the life of the children before we can wisely teach them.

The thoughtful teacher remembers this truth and directs her work accordingly. Instead of rushing with headlong zeal into the routine of reading, writing, and number — under the impulsion of the Course of Study, and the memory of classes which failed to " pass " — she makes haste slowly, and devotes the first days of the term to lessons which help to reveal the experience of the children. Observation of and talks about common things ; conversations which lead the children to tell what they can do, or like to do ; story telling ; picture drawing ; — these afford opportunity for expression, and serve to show the teacher something of her pupils' attainments, and the line of their interests as well. Meanwhile, they are becoming accustomed to the schoolroom routine, and so emerge from the period in which they gazed, dazed and dumb, at the many marvels with which this new school world is crowded. They come to know the teacher as their friend, and they become free and confident in her presence. Thus the true

THE ART OF READING. 17

atmosphere of the schoolroom is created — the only atmosphere in which wholesome and natural teaching and learning can thrive.

This is not a prodigal misuse of time. It is the part of thrift to so spend in the beginning, for the returns are evident in the ease and readiness with which pupils and teacher afterward work together — the value of every lesson being enhanced by the mutual good will and understanding.

The school differs from the home and the kindergarten in that its allotted tasks are evidently determined by a motive and plan outside the child's comprehension. In many cases this must be so. The lessons which involve the mastery of the symbols used in reading, writing and number, or the drill and practice necessary to attain skill in music or drawing or writing, have no self-evident goal for the child. So many lines, so many letters, so many problems, he attempts, because the teacher says so, and in his new universe the teacher is supreme. At home he has always chosen more or less; so, too, in the kindergarten his interest and choice determined the story or the game or the topic of conversation. He has delighted in building houses, modeling balls, weaving mats, playing games — and all, so far as he knew, for his own immediate pleasure and accomplishment. Other results, to him unknown, were of course secured. He builded better than he knew. But in every case he rejoiced in some immediate accomplishment which he desired.

In too many cases the decreed exercises of the school are meaningless and purposeless to the beginner. Such exercises easily degenerate into dull and fruitless routine, indifferent and profitless to teacher and pupil alike. To arouse desire and awaken conscious motive is the teacher's most important work, and in teaching reading it should receive first consideration. She, therefore, after securing such freedom and coöperation as promise a fertile soil for her seed-planting, calls the children about her to explain the purpose of the lessons which will fill their days.

Perhaps she reads to them a story which they like, a new story which they have never heard. When she reaches the interesting climax she pauses to say, "I haven't time to read the rest of the story now. How I wish you could read! Then you might take the book and read the story yourselves. Would you not like to learn to read, so that you could read stories like these?"

In Hugh Miller's graphic description of his childhood experience in reading, this element of purpose and desire is strongly emphasized. "The process of learning and acquiring had been a dark one," he says, recalling his struggles with letters and syllables. He "slowly mastered" these "in humble confidence in the awful wisdom of the schoolmistress, not knowing whither it tended," — when (as a member of the Bible Class — "in the highest form") his mind "awoke to the meaning of that most delightful of all narratives, the story of Joseph. Was there ever such a discovery made before?"

Such testimony might be repeated a thousand times over, by our pupils of to-day — if they were able to describe their common experience.

It was the first vision of the goal that gave meaning, motive, and conscious gladness to Hugh Miller's study. Such motive and such meaning should pervade the earliest lessons in reading, and should be consciously recognized by pupil as well as teacher. We repeat then: the teacher's first effort, after becoming acquainted with her children, is to awaken this conscious desire to read, and to secure intelligent coöperation in her exercises.

One teacher suggests writing upon the board some sentence which has been whispered to her by the children, and then calling an older child from another room to read the secret. This is done again and again, until the children are eager to share the power which their comrade possesses, and turn gladly to the tasks required of them, that they may the sooner reach their goal.

There is a wide difference between such teaching and the routine drill which does not enlist the child's desire. The enthusiastic bicyclist would smile if asked to exchange his morning ride to the city for an hour's exercise upon a fixed "bicycle exerciser" in the back hall. Nor could the most skilful pedagogue convince him that the exercise involved in making the wheel go round is as valuable as the spin which carries him to his destination, through the fresh morning air, along roads bordered with flowered fields. Yet the contrast is no more marked than that between the task of the syllable-pronouncer, who obediently performs his meaningless labor, and that of the child who, with conscious and earnest desire, sets himself to learn to read.

In order to give some sense of immediate achievement, the first lessons should be in sentences, expressing thoughts in which the children are interested.

This is Kate.
Kate can read.
Kate has a book.
Read to me, Kate.
Kate can read.
I can read, too.
Kate has a book.
I have a book, too.
See Kate's book!
See my book!

Kate has a doll.
I have a doll, too.
Kate has a kitty.
I have a dog.
Kate likes her doll.
I like my dog.
See my dog!
See Kate's little kitty!
Come, little Kitty.
Come to me, Kitty.

The object of these preparatory lessons is to give some consciousness of the purpose of reading, and some sense of achievement. The sentences are the children's, obtained in a conversation concerning Kate, who is an older pupil, or some pictured child. The sentence is the unit, and is read by the teacher. The children repeat the sentence after her reading.

Of course these first efforts are not reading. They simply represent the children's memory of the teacher's words and tone. Often, when asked to read alone, the child dashes at the wrong sentence with his pointer, which vainly wanders in search of the right one. But just as the frequent observation of the loved story in the picture book not only fixes the words in their order, but enables the young listener to find some of them upon the page, so, by repetition of these first sentences, the words are at last held in the mind, and are recognized in new places and under new relations. The attentive eye will recognize the new words, first in their wonted place in the sentence, then when isolated. At first the words selected for repetition and recognition are those which present fewest difficulties. Not by any means the shortest words — as a, is, too — but the meaningful words, the nouns, and adjectives, and verbs which denote action. **Kate, book, doll, dog, kitty** — these are the first and easiest, in the lessons written above. Later, **see** and **likes**, with **can read**. Later still, **I have, this is** — while **is** and **a** will not be emphasized as units until the eyes have been trained to distinguish more readily, and the words have become familiar through constant repetition.

Such lessons should continue for several weeks, introducing the various dear and oft-seen objects of the child's environment, and the actions with which he has long been familiar. The sentences should be worth reading, and grouped in coherent paragraphs. Drill in recognizing the words should follow the sentence reading, in every day's lesson.

When the children can recognize at sight a vocabulary of one hundred or two hundred words, they should begin to compare them, and to place in groups those which are alike in sound. For example: **book, look,** and **brook,** are known, — **red** and **fed, cat, hat,** and **pat** — **Fan, ran, can,** and **Dan.** Placed in lists, their similarity is evident.

book	fed	cat	Fan
look	red	hat	ran
brook		pat	can
			Dan
took	*bed*	*sat*	*man*

Some one volunteers to increase the list, adding **took, bed, sat,** and **man.** Here is the beginning of the analysis of words into their sounds, and with this lesson a new feature appears in our word study.

Such lessons in sentence reading as have been suggested, if continued long enough and with sufficient discretion on the part of the teacher, might enable a class to read independently — for, even without the teacher's direction, obvious likenesses and differences in words are noted by the children, and rules are deduced therefrom. But the mastery of a large vocabulary is readily secured only through attention to the common laws of pronunciation, and familiarity with the sound units. Thus far every word has been presented as a new unit. Now the children should learn that these words are like many others in form, and that the pronunciation of one serves as a key to the many. Knowing **book,** all monosyllables ending in *ook* can at once enter their vocabulary of recognizable words; knowing **Fan,** all monosyllables with the *an* ending are known. The missing factor is the knowledge of the sounds of the separate letters, which are initials in these group words — m-an F-an c-an r-an t-an p-an. At this juncture these sounds should be taught.

There has been some question among teachers as to the time for teaching sounds of the letters. It is wise to defer this teaching until the children have acquired some little facility in reading, and understand its purpose, that their work may not be approached from the mechanical side solely. Again, the vocabulary which the children already know reveals the groups of similar words and suggests the wisdom of analysis and classification. And further, the too early attempt to study the lists of similar words and to select and emphasize them for use in reading, drives the children at once to their most difficult task. It is much easier to recognize **Hiawatha** and **arrow**, because they are long and different, and seem hard, than to name promptly the elusive **can**, **ran**, and **tan**, which seem so easy and yet are so nearly alike as to be formidable obstacles to the success of the untrained observer. The climax of objection is reached when we cite the tendency to make sentences solely for the sake of using certain words, thus destroying the element of thought value in the sentence. "Does the fat rat see the cat on the mat?" is far more difficult for a child than is "Hiawatha lived in a wigwam with old Nokomis" — for the reasons above named.

The mastery of words is an essential element in learning to read. Our common mistake is, not that we do such work too well, but that we make it the final aim of the reading lesson, and lead the children to feel that they can read when they are merely able to pronounce words. Perhaps lack of careful attention to the form of words is quite as serious a mistake, for it results in carelessness in reading.

The study of form and of sound should be associated, but attention to sound alone should precede any attempt to master the form as suggesting sound. Children should be taught to recognize and to distinguish sounds, to repeat them accurately, to speak them distinctly, before they are taught to copy the single characters which represent these sounds. To hear, to repeat, to compare, to distinguish sounds, should be the order of the instruction.

Careless speech and indistinct articulation often arise from imperfect hearing, or indifferent attention to what is said. Children should be trained in the early lessons to hear, and to repeat, *exactly what is said.* The repetition is a test of the child's hearing. Begin with short sentences. Speak them clearly, in a moderate voice, requiring the children to repeat after *once* hearing. Gradually increase the length of sentence, but do not increase the volume of voice; speak distinctly, and expect the children to be attentive enough to hear an ordinary tone; teach them to respond in the same tone, with clear articulation. Continue this exercise until a long sentence can be accurately returned; then pronounce lists of words beginning with letters which demand careful articulation. When these have been mastered, draw attention to initial sounds, and then to the letters which represent them. Work with these until every letter suggests its sounds to the pupils, whether in a new or in a familiar word. With little children, the sound should be taught first in connection with initial letters always. A successful device consists in allowing each pupil to represent a certain sound. If the sound is the initial sound in his own name, it will be easy for the children to remember. Thus — John can always suggest the sound of j, Mary the sound of m, Peter the sound of p, and so on. A class of children aided in this way will master the sounds of the letters in a very short time.

Having learned, through the initials, the sounds which various letters represent, the next step will be to analyze phonosyllables into their sounds. Select first those containing short vowels, in order to avoid the difficulty of the silent letter. The preliminary drill with the initials will have made this step an easy one to take.

Whenever a type word is represented, as — black, for example, the children should be taught to suggest other words which rhyme with the pattern, as — crack, back, lack, etc. If in every such case the common element is studied and mastered, in a few weeks the children will become possessors of a large vocabulary, whose basis is the few common words which they have studied. Every type word will stand for a list of words similar in form.

This study of sounds should continue through at least the first five school years. After analyzing any word into its separate sounds, the children should be required to name other known words which resemble the one studied. This will tend to a habit of classification which will recall the known word, which helps the student to master the new one.

Diacritical marks are a help in mastering new words, if the key words have been studied in connection with the marks. They are needed also in consulting the dictionary for pronunciation. They should be taught only when necessary to the pronunciation. In older classes, after the use of the dictionary becomes necessary, a complete list should be mastered. It is a mistake to insist upon diacritical marking when the children can pronounce accurately without. I remember hearing a teacher chide a pupil for reading a sentence before she had time to mark the vowels, but, since the child could and did read without such help, the marking was evidently unnecessary. It serves as a means to an end, and should be dispensed with when the end can be reached without such artificial aid.

As a matter of fact, every child refers a new word back to a similar word with which he has become familiar. Thus — **black**, once mastered, serves as a key to **nack, crack, quack,** etc. The only elements in these words are the final element **ack** and the initial sounds. If a child hesitates with a new word, help him to refer at once to the type word which he has already mastered. Instead of pronouncing the new word for him, insist upon his using for himself his own stock of knowledge. Help him only where he cannot help himself. If he forms the habit of referring the unknown to the kindred known, he will become independent in study. For example — to a six-years-old child the word blacksmith may, at first sight, appear formidable. Separated into its parts and referred to the simple words already mastered, the child conquers the newcomer, and adds it to his list of servants. He is endowed with new strength, because he has mastered something which seemed to him hard. Such conquests, often repeated, lead to strength and independence. In many cases, it is wise to leave a child to wrestle with a word which at first sight he fails to master. Of course this process is unwise if he has no experience to which he can refer for help. Guess-work will never take the place of thought, and a child should not be driven to guess at the pronunciation, but every attempt should be based upon something which he has been taught in former lessons. Such practice will lead to thoughtful self-help.

This work may be facilitated by many devices. We have seen classes hunting for new words beginning with a given sound, as eagerly as if they were playing hide and seek. Or with the utmost enjoyment they have made lists of words beginning with chosen sounds; or matched pairs of words which rhymed. But their most valuable exercise is that in which the old familiar word of their first vocabulary is made the key which unlocks the new.

Now, when a new word is presented, the teacher no longer pronounces it for the children, but asks instead, "What word helps you to pronounce it?" **Bright** is not a new word, because the children know **light**, remember the sound of **br**, and put their two bits of knowledge together to meet the new emergency. They do for themselves what the teacher has heretofore done for them.

A most helpful form of word study, which is suitable for desk work, is making lists of words containing the same sound. It strengthens the habit of classification, and helps in spelling and in the recognition of new words.

The most difficult work for children appears in words which are spelled alike and pronounced differently, or in words pronounced alike and spelled differently, or in the various equivalents of the same sound which our language affords. **Chair, their, where,** etc. suggest the problems of this nature. This work should be introduced not earlier than the third or fourth year. It should come in connection with the spelling lesson, and not with the reading. The mastery of these difficulties in English spelling doubtless requires many months of careful teaching.

It must not be forgotten that children are hindered and not helped by any attempt to spell by sound, words which are unique in spelling. **Through,** for example, should be learned by sight, and not by sound. **Beautiful, tongue, physique** — may illustrate this group. The eye, and not the ear, must be depended upon in the mastery of such words. Care should be taken to develop the habit of accurate attention through the eye as well as the ear. Any attempt to mark the sounds in these words increases the labor without increasing facility. If the teacher makes a careful classification of the ordinary words which frequently recur in the reading lesson, she will discover the class which must be mastered by sight. Out of the remainder she can make lists which include the ordinary type sounds. The study of these lists will reduce the labor of word mastery to its minimum, and the habit of comparison developed through this study will go far to make the children independent in the pronunciation of new words.

For diacritical marks and correct pronunciation, the teacher is referred to the standard dictionaries. It should not be forgotten that the teacher's pronunciation is a guide to the pupil. She needs a quick ear and the careful judgment which will render her a safe guide. The familiar rule should direct her practice. When in doubt, consult the dictionary.

Note the value of this word mastery. The pupil fast becomes independent of the teacher, and ready to master the page for himself. Note, also, that this power becomes his in proportion to the teacher's purpose to make him self-helpful, and her skill in finding the connecting link between the new knowledge and the old.

It is self-evident that this plan can be pursued only when the words are amenable to common phonic laws. **Cough**, and its congeners, should be named as new wholes. So with all words which follow no rule, and must be pronounced by substitution. No time should be lost by attempting a method which has no excuse for being, in such cases. In its place, as a help to the mastery of groups of kindred words, it is invaluable. Out of place, it is bad.

Two elements of learning to read have been presented here: sentence reading and word mastery. Of the study of the meaning of the words and the development of the power of imagination we shall speak elsewhere.

Part II.

THE FIRST YEAR IN READING.

SUGGESTIONS TO TEACHERS.

Part II.

CHAPTER III.

THE FIRST YEAR IN READING.

Suggestions to Teachers.

I.

THE FIRST LESSON WITH THE BOOK.

IT is assumed that the teacher whose class is undertaking the initial lessons in reading has already prepared the way for the book, by language lessons and by reading from the blackboard. The children have gained some idea of the purpose of reading, and can already read a number of simple sentences which have been written upon the board or paper. Now comes the happy day when the book is placed in their hands.

This should be considered by both teacher and pupil a most eventful day. When Mrs. Wesley taught her children their letters, she dressed them in their best clothes, and they sat in state, in happy anticipation of the great event. Doubtless their rapid acquisition of the alphabet was largely due to the deep impression which the mother thus made upon them. Commonplace as the routine lesson may appear to the teacher, she should not forget that the first study of the book opens the door into book-land for the children. She should make the day a happy one, and emphasize this new beginning which points so hopefully to future achievement.

The class awaits the distribution of the new books with eager anticipation. A few words from the teacher suggest to the children the value of the book, the care which should be exercised in handling it, the virtue of clean hands, the objection to marks and blots, curled edges and torn pages. But when the treasures are once in the hands of the pupils, she allows them to turn the pages at their own sweet will, to look at the pictures, and to express their delight in their new possession. Perhaps she calls the little ones about her and shows them how to open and to hold the book, how to turn the page, how to find new pages. She talks with them about some of the pictures in which they are interested, and then bids them search for words which they already know.

It is much more difficult for little children to read from the printed page, meanwhile holding the book and "keeping their place," than to read the same sentence from the board as it has just appeared beneath the teacher's crayon. It is the part of wisdom, therefore, to acquaint the children with the few words upon the first pages of the book, before they are introduced to these pages. Until the manipulation of the book becomes easy, and the pupils have learned to find and to follow the lines upon the page, the sentences should present the least possible difficulty in themselves. It is supposed, then, that the children who take the First Reader into their hands have already read from the board the sentences found upon the first ten pages, at least, and know the words and phrases which are included in these sentences. If this is the case, they will read all that is found upon these pages in the first two or three days after the book is given them.

II.

THE FIRST VOCABULARY.

The first twenty-four pages of the First Reader of "Stepping Stones to Literature" contain lessons which are intended to be mastered by the children with the help of the teacher, by the so-called "word and sentence" method, without any attempt at phonic analysis. The reasons for this mode of proceeding have been given in the previous chapter. During these lessons, therefore, the children will acquire little power to master new words independently. Their attention has not yet been called to the structure of the individual word. Stress has been laid, and intentionally, upon the meaning of the word, the form of the sentence, and the thought expressed by it. It may be a simple matter to present to children a dozen things at once, but it does not follow that they understand everything which is presented to them. The writer has seen so much difficulty in reading that arose from the child's complete misconception of the object of reading, so much crude, helpless, and blundering work due to the complete lack of meaning in the exercise, that she has come to firmly believe that the first and most important duty of the teacher of reading is to emphasize its one aim — thought-getting. To this end, she is willing even to lose time (or seem to lose time) in the first few weeks of the child's school life, in the effort to give a clear conception of this purpose, rather than to fix in the mind of both pupil and teacher, as a goal, the power of word pronouncing.

Therefore, no attempt has been made to select for the vocabulary of these first pages words which are alike in sound. Nouns have been chosen for their intrinsic interest. They name familiar objects which all children like; the verbs, as far as possible, express action; the adjectives are descriptive. The forms of the words are varied. It is easier to distinguish words which are markedly different from one another than to recognize those which present slight differences merely. **Do you like bread and milk, Fan?** is easier to read than **Does the fat cat see the rat on the mat?** Furthermore, to insist upon a phonic vocabulary, at this stage, would so limit the range of sentences as to make the lessons mechanical, and largely eliminate any free expression of thought.

The words used, however, are such as will serve in the future as type words, in the various phonic lists which the children must learn. The study of phonics is simply postponed, that it may be subordinate to the chief end in reading, and the teacher is asked to use these first pages without effort to emphasize that phase of word mastery. That will come later, in its rightful place. Meanwhile, the child is unconsciously mastering a vocabulary which will serve as a basis for his classification and analysis, later.

III.

THE FIRST SERIES OF LESSONS.

Page eleven represents Ben running after a ball. He has been introduced before as **our dog**. The first sentence presents nothing new. The action in the picture suggests animation, and the children will read in an animated fashion. The exclamation point intimates this to the teacher. It is not intended for the children, and should not be mentioned unless the children ask questions about it.

Tr. Look at Ben's face. Do you think he is a cross dog? What kind of dog is Ben?
Ch. He is a good dog.

Tr. What is he doing?
Ch. He is running.
Tr. See him run! Tell him to run.
Ch. Run, Ben!
Tr. What is he trying to do?
Ch. He is trying to get the ball.
Tr. Tell him to get it.
Ch. Get the ball!

The children read these sentences with such expression as they would use if talking to their mates about Ben, or urging the dog to run. The next sentence, **He can get the ball**, presents no new word, and therefore is easy. Let the children dig it out for themselves, going back to earlier sentences to refresh their memory, if it is necessary. Let them read the first two words of the next sentence — **Ben likes** : — these, too, are familiar.

Tr. What does he like to do?
Ch. He likes to run, he likes to jump.

The **to** is not emphasized; it is written with the **run**. **To run and jump** may be taught as one phrase, just as **bread and milk** has been. And is becoming familiar to the children now, though it is meaningless to them; and **to** will soon become familiar, by repetition. Meanwhile, it should not be emphasized in the first lesson.

Tr. Ben likes to run and jump.
Can you run? Can you jump?

Do you like to run? Do you like to jump?
Let me see you run. Let me see you jump.
What can you do?
Ch. I can run and jump.
Tr. You can do what Ben can do. Can Ben do everything that you can do? What can you do?
Ch. I can read.
Tr. Can Ben read?

If this lesson is presented upon the board before the children attempt to read it from the book, abundant repetition may be provided which will help to fix the words in mind. Such word lessons are indispensable to the early teaching of reading. They afford opportunity for frequent repetition, with variety. Any book lesson in permanent form is quickly memorized by the children, and a sentence once memorized is useless as a test. Whatever book or lesson is used at this stage, the teacher should supplement it by rapid and varied lessons upon the board. These have the added value of appearing newly made before the eyes of the children. The freshness always adds to the interest.

This is Ben.
Ben is our dog.
See our dog! See Ben!
Ben is a good dog.
I like Ben.
Ben likes me.

See Ben run! See him run!
Run, Ben! Get the ball!
Run and get the ball.
He can get the ball.
Ben likes to run.
He likes to jump.
I like to run.
I like to jump.
Ben and I can run and jump.
I can run. Ben can run.
I can jump. Ben can jump.
I can read. Can Ben read?

Page twelve contains no new word except **she**. This word will not be emphasized; it simply takes the place of **kitty**, and naturally slips into its appointed place. It will be repeated often enough to insure recognition. Like is — our — my — the — to — and — it is a necessary link in the sentence, but has not such meaning as to readily fix the attention of the child. These sentences may be multiplied as in the previous lesson.

This is my kitty.
See my kitty!
She likes to run.
She likes to jump.
Ben and Kitty like to run and jump.

She is a good kitty.
She likes me.
I can run, Kitty.
I can jump.
Run, Kitty, run.
Run and jump, Kitty!
See me run! See me jump!
See me, Kitty!
Can Kitty see Ben?
Can Ben see Kitty?

Page thirteen contains no new word. This is — she is — I like — can you — I see — should be repeated over and over, in sentences, until they present no difficulty. Supplementary sentences may be made as before.

IV.

SILENT READING.

On page sixteen, Silent Reading is proposed, its object being not simply to test the children's perception of the thought, but to help them to realize that the chief object of reading is to enable them to get the meaning of the sentences. Their answers should be spoken in sentences.

Yes, I see Kitty.
Kitty can jump.
No, she does not eat grass.
Yes, Ben likes bread and milk.
Meat is good for children to eat.
Dogs like meat, too.
Grass is good for cows to eat.

Multiply these exercises. Write the questions upon slips of paper, distribute them to the children, and ask them to read the question and to give the answer in turn. Such an exercise affords variety which is always pleasing to children, and, further, serves as a test of their power to get the meaning of the question.

Questions for Silent Reading, in connection with the first twenty-four pages:

Have you a ball?
Have you a blue ball?
Is your ball little?

Where is your ball?
Do you like to play ball?
Can Ben play ball?
Do you like dogs?
Have you a dog?
Does your dog like to play?
Can you run?
Do you like to run?
Can Ben jump?
Does Ben like to jump?
Does Fan like Ben?
Can Fan play with Ben?
Does Fan like Kitty?
Can Kitty play with the ball?
Does Baby like bread and milk?
Can Baby eat bread?
Can Baby drink milk?
Can Baby see Fan?
Is Fan good to the baby?
Is old Fan in the field?
Can you run in the field?
Can you play in the field?
Do you like to play in the field?

Can you play in the brook?
Do you like to play in the brook?
Old Fan drinks from the brook.
Can you drink water from the brook?
Do you see Fan and Baby?
Do you see Ned?
Can Ned play ball?
Has Ned a good ball?
Does Ned like to play with Ben?
Can Ned milk Fan?
Can you find Ned's ball?
Is Ned's ball like your ball?

V.

SENTENCES TO BE COMPLETED.

On page twenty-four, an exercise is introduced which may be made very profitable. Obviously, no one can fill the blanks in the sentences without first being able to pronounce the written words and give their meaning. Such exercises, then, serve as a test of the children's mastery of the words used, and also afford a pleasing variety for seat work. The exercise seems like a game to the children, and they enter into it with the spirit of play. Cards, or slips, upon which such broken sentences are written, may be made very useful, both for seat work and for varying the class exercise in reading.

Incomplete sentences to be completed by the children:

Baby —— old Fan.
Fan gives —— to Baby.
Fan —— water.
Baby has a ——ball.
Ned plays in the ——.
He likes to play ——.
Ben is —— dog.
He can —— and ——.
Our Kate —— Ben.
Kate plays with ——.
Ben —— my ball.
Ben —— with Kitty.

Kate likes —— and ——.
Kate can ——.
I like ——.
I like to drink ——.
Fan eats ——.
Kate eats —— and ——.
Kitty eats ——.
Ben likes —— and ——.
Ned can play ——.
Fan is a —— cow.
Ned is a —— boy.
Ben is a —— dog.

VI.

DIFFICULT WORDS.

The words which really hinder the children in their reading, are the little words having no appreciable meaning to the young learners. Prepositions, conjunctions, interjections, copulative verbs, articles and expletives are necessary links in the sentence, but are difficult to master as units. These words should be taught in connection with the nouns or verbs with which they are associated in the sentence. Constant repetition makes them familiar. After they are recognized with some ease and readiness, lists should be made upon the board, and at the period of word study these lists should be repeated by the children until immediate recognition and accuracy in pronunciation are assured. The common mistake is to suppose that the longer the word, the more difficult the mastery. The teacher's experience, however, goes to prove that it is the little word which causes stumbling and prevents clear recognition of the thought. The teacher should carefully note the words which occasion stumbling, and, having selected those which frequently recur in the reading lessons and therefore must necessarily be learned, should give time to drill upon this selected list. A chart may be prepared, and a daily repetition required, or the lists may be placed upon cards, which are distributed to the children to be used in a variety of ways, as the teacher may direct. The point is, that, while these seemingly unimportant words are without emphasis in the reading, they should receive particular attention in the word study and drill, so that the ordinary stumbling and hesitation may be prevented.

VII.

THE BEGINNING OF PHONICS.

On page twenty-five, lessons upon the sounds of the letters make their appearance. Reference to the chapter upon THE ART OF READING will show the relation of these lessons to the other exercises in reading. It is time now for the children to know the sounds of the letters, that they may help themselves in the pronunciation of new words. The device which has been adopted to aid them in this exercise is partly old and partly new. Pages 25, 26, 27, and 28 contain a child's table of reference. The letters are arranged in alphabetical order. With each letter appears a word chosen because that letter indicates its initial sound. In pronouncing a word, the child must first make the sound for which the letter stands. The short sounds of the vowels have been used because they occur most frequently in the child's early vocabulary in reading. The pictures have been placed beside the word to add interest, and to help the children in their first rendering of the word. Nouns have been chosen, in every instance. The words in this list are not intended to be **sounded** by the children. Their phonic analysis will extend in this case only to the initial letter.

The pupils should be drilled upon this list until they can give the sound of every letter without reference to the table. Should they fail to give the proper sound in their later work, they should be referred to the table to find it, thus beginning self-help in the use of books. The teacher who adopts a different vocabulary for the early lessons may make a table which will be more helpful to herself, but the writer is convinced that such help at this stage is very valuable. Its worth appears in proportion as the children are made to depend upon themselves in their exercises, and to refer to the table when they need help. The sounding or phonic analysis of words which admit of such analysis, should become a part of their exercise in word study, at this stage, and the children should be urged to use their new knowledge in pronouncing new-words, depending as far as possible upon themselves, and asking the teacher's aid only as a last resort.

Sounds of the Letters.

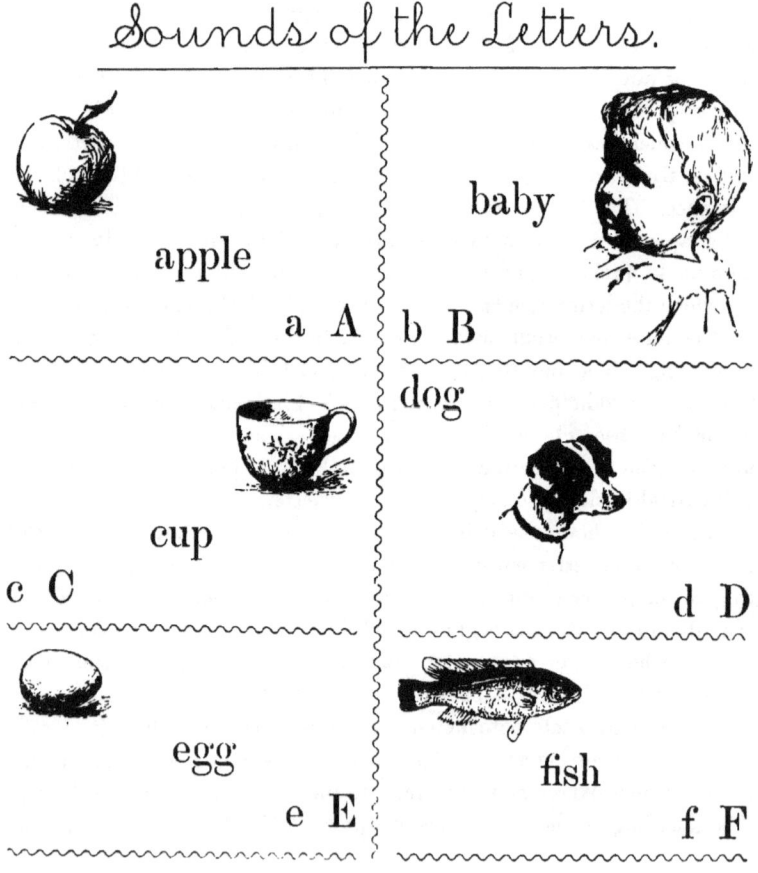

apple

a A   b B

dog

cup

c C   d D

egg   fish

e E   f F

VIII.

THE USE OF RHYMES.

Pages twenty-nine and thirty introduce exercises in word study in which the rhyme is called into service. Observation of children's early use of picture books teaches us that many young readers learn to recognize words through their place in the rhyme. Who does not remember reading the rhymed story to the eager child-listener, who followed the words upon the page with his index finger, and named aloud each word at the end of the line? It was not long before he could recognize all the rhymed words at the end of the line, and, later, he became able to name prominent words in the line, reciting from memory, and pointing to the words in order, as he recited. The writer has often made use of this natural tendency of the children, in teaching classes to read, and has found that many words which would otherwise seem difficult to learn, are easily acquired and added to the child's reading vocabulary if they are found in memorized rhymes. The device is mechanical, of course. It simply makes use of something which the child likes to do, and turns it to account in the acquisition of the early vocabulary.

On page twenty-nine, appears the familiar rhyme:

> One, two, three, four, five,
> I caught a hare alive.
> Six, seven, eight, nine, ten,
> I let him go again.

Most of the children have already memorized this nursery jingle. If they have not, it will be quickly committed to memory. After they know it — *not before* — let them point to the words as they read them, one by one; then ask them to find the words, skipping about, without regard to order; recognize the same words upon the top or bottom of the page, and afterwards require them in their busy work to write the words beside the corresponding figures. Most of the words will recur frequently in the child's reading; the others need not be emphasized until their recurrence makes this necessary. The figures should be utilized at once in finding the pages of the Reader.

On page thirty, the exercise is carried still farther. The well-known rhyme, "Jack and Jill," appears, with appropriate illustration. The children are supposed to have memorized the rhyme before attempting the word study. Having memorized it, they find the different words in the rhyme, from their position, naming them one by one. After they can readily find them, new words are introduced which rhyme with the words found in the lesson. Here is an occasion for turning back to the alphabetical list, in order to discover the sound of the initial letter. The child who knows the word **Jill** and knows the alphabetical sounds, ought to be able to pronounce fill for himself. **Tell** ought to be easily conquered by the child who knows **fell**; **let** is pronounced easily after **get** is known; **lame** is easy after **came** is mastered, and so on.

The exercise is intended to be suggestive of a type of word study which is always fraught with interest to the children. Teachers will note that the words which are made useful in the rhymes are the so-called type-words which appear as representatives of a family, or class of words. **Tumbling** and **after** are ignored, but **went** stands for the group which includes **bent** — **sent** — **dent** — **lent** — **pent** — **rent** — **tent** — **scent**, etc. and therefore is an acquisition not to be despised. It is hoped that the teacher will make frequent use of such exercises, placing upon the board the familiar nursery rhymes, and underlining the words which may serve the children as indicated in this exercise.

It should perhaps be said that these two pages afford material for several lessons, and that the teacher should not attempt to complete the indicated study at one period.

IX

READING AND DRAWING

Several of the lessons in the First Reader are accompanied by outlined sketches which are intended to serve as material for seat work. Any teacher of little children will understand how they may be used. It may be well to advise in this connection a free use of the pencil in illustrating sentences. Children are ordinarily very ready to express their thoughts with the pencil, and their drawings may be made very helpful to the teacher. They reveal the child's notion of the thought in the sentence, and often show his mistaken ideas, thus giving the teacher an opportunity to correct them. They are a fair indication, too, of the pupil's real interest, and always deserve the teacher's careful study. Whenever the lesson will afford such opportunity, the children should be encouraged to draw the picture suggested to them by the sentence.

Old Fan is in the field.
My ball is under the table.
Baby has a cup of milk.
Kitty likes to play with Ben.
Jack and Jill went up the hill.
The mother hen has five chickens.
Our house is a farmhouse.
Jack can draw a load of hay.
I like to ride on the hay.
Ben can swim in the water.

The robin has a nest in the tree.
Ned found the robin's nest.
Mary had a little lamb.
It followed her to school one day.
The little flower grows in the field.
The little fish swims in the sea.
The bear lives in the woods.
Jack can sail a boat.
The boat sails on the water.
Jack's home is near the sea.
Mary's lamb eats from her hand.

After a limited vocabulary has been mastered, the teacher can make frequent use of such exercises, for silent reading at the desks, the children reading the sentences to themselves and drawing the pictures which they represent. They invariably enjoy such exercises, and the pencil interpretation is often more satisfactory than the oral reading.

X.

GROUPS OF SIMILAR WORDS.

Word Study upon page thirty-two uses the words of the lesson to extend the vocabulary. **Smile** becomes **smiles** by the addition of **s**; **speak** becomes **speaks**; **take** becomes **takes**, and **hand** is changed to **hands**. Let such exercises in word drill be multiplied until the children become able to pronounce a group of related words, after having the single one presented to them. All regular plurals can be taught in this way, after the singular has been presented: so with the various derivatives which occur in adjective or verb forms. Walk, walks, walking, sidewalk; speak, speaks, speaker, speaking, — may serve to suggest the possibilities of this exercise.

As far as possible, the exercises in word study which are intended to increase the vocabulary should be referred back to the known words which occur in the reading lessons, so that the children may be enabled to use those words as the key to the other groups, and to search in the present treasure for the word which will unlock the new sentence to them. This habit of working for themselves, of depending upon themselves, is invaluable, and it should be developed, even at the expense of seemingly slow progress in the beginning. To pronounce a word for the child is quicker work than to help him pronounce it for himself, but it is not serviceable for the next lesson; while the power acquired by his own doing makes him master of countless pages.

Throughout the book, occasional lessons in word study have been suggested, whenever a list of words has been given with endings like a representative found in the lesson. These are simply typical, and it is well to use other words in the same way. Whenever the children build such lists in independent exercises, without the immediate direction of the teacher, they should read them afterward, in order that she may judge whether the work has been done intelligently. The exercise is much more valuable when it is thus tested.

The third column for word study on page thirty-five includes some of the words of indefinite meaning which have been referred to as difficult. Included in this list, we shall find he written with both capital and small letter. All teachers of beginners are familiar with the difficulty presented when the capital is introduced in a word which has been hitherto one beginning with the small letter. An excellent exercise to overcome this difficulty, is a drill in writing, beginning the words in both ways. First begin with the small letter, and then with the capital. Inasmuch as any word may present this difficulty when it occurs at the beginning of a sentence, the trouble is a frequent one, and such drill will go far to remove it.

Pages thirty-six and thirty-seven continue such lists of words. It will be understood that many of these words will never appear in the vocabulary of the lessons. These exercises are intended merely for word study.

XI.

LANGUAGE LESSONS WITH READING.

In another chapter, the relation of the language lessons to the reading lessons is discussed at some length. The lesson upon this page presents an opportunity for an observation lesson which will go far to increase the interest in the reading, and will, furthermore, supply material for many reading lessons. Obviously, a talk upon birds will bring to the minds of the children whatever knowledge they have gained on the subject, and will show the teacher whether any pupils are unprepared for the lesson. These lessons were intended both for the children who know the robin and for those who do not, but in the latter case the preparatory lessons should be given in which the children do observe the robin, the nest, and the egg, or approach this as nearly as possible. Several primary teachers whom the writer has known well are accustomed to take their pupils into the woods to observe the birds. Where this is impossible, the English sparrow is omnipresent and can serve as a type for the city bird life. The children watch the sparrow: tell how large he is; what his color is; what he can do; what they have seen him do; where he builds his nest; how he builds it; of what material he makes it; how he feeds his little birds; how they beg for food; what the sparrows have for breakfast; what they use instead of knife, fork, spoon, and plate; how the sparrow's home differs from the home of the children, etc. Such observation lessons give the children a fund of material for expression, and the lessons upon the board are very valuable at this time. All the knowledge gained in regard to the sparrow will serve to interest them in regard to the robin, whose picture is presented on page thirty-eight (as well as on page fifty-nine) and who returns again and again to speak for himself.

Such a preparation for the lesson will help the pupils to enter upon the reading with zest and interest. Their questions will be real questions, and the answers will tell what they know is true. Not the least profitable element in the exercise will be the sympathy with bird life which is developed by the preliminary lessons, and continued in the reading. Already the children are beginning to read something which has a message for them, and they enter upon it with a spirit which is entirely different from that which accompanies the reading of lessons that are made purely for the sake of including the words of their past vocabulary.

In the lessons upon pages thirty-eight and thirty-nine, new words are rare. Such as do occur are repeated, and are easy to master because they are necessary to the meaning of the text. **Touch** is a word which should not be taught by sound, at this stage. **Good morning** will be taught as a single phrase; it will return again and again. **Please** will also become an old friend. **Coming** should be associated with come, which the children have already learned. It will be easy to increase this lesson indefinitely, because the vocabulary is full enough to admit of such development.

XII.

THE SUBJECTS OF THE LESSONS.

Reference was made in the preceding section to the language lesson which should accompany the reading. It will be noted that the subjects of the lessons thus far have been those with which nearly all children are familiar. The cat, the dog, the horse, the cow, the bird, the baby, are friends near and dear to most children. They have been purposely selected because of their inherent interest, as the children already know these old friends and like to talk about them.

Page forty introduces the home, with the mother and sister, the garden, the flowers, — and leads the children to a comparison between their home and the home of the birds; the mother love which they know, and the love which the bird mother shows for her children. A wise teacher will make much of this exercise.

On page forty-three the well known story of Mary and her little lamb appears. This is intended to be used in the same manner as the nursery rhymes which have preceded. Some of the words as **lingered** and **eager**, do not reappear in the children's vocabulary. They are necessary for this reading merely. The lesson is not intended to be read before memorizing, but to be memorized before reading. The exercise serves purely as an exercise in word study. Such words as lingered and eager should be dropped out of the drill exercise as soon as they have served their purpose in this lesson.

The exercise on page forty-four is intended as a test of silent reading, the pupils being required to read silently and to give the answers aloud.

XIII.

THE STUDY OF PICTURES.

The lessons in the next five pages speak of the different homes of different children. Here is an opportunity for language lessons, illustrated by pictures which will give the children some notion of the lives of other children. The boy who lives by the sea, the one who lives on the farm, and the child whose home is in the city, are contrasted, and their occupations are suggested. Pictures which are drawn from nature, or which interpret life under these varying conditions, should be brought to the class, to help the pupils to get more from their reading. Pictures of the farmhouse, of farmyards and the animals to be found there; pictures of men plowing, or sowing, or reaping; scenes in the meadow, in the woods, on the hill, by the brook, — all these serve as material for both language and reading lessons, at this stage. If the teacher is fortunate enough to have a large number of First Readers at hand, so that she can secure this material without making it, here is opportunity to use them wisely. But the best possible material is that which she makes upon the board at the time of the little children's expressed interest in the subject they have been discussing. Just such lessons should help to interpret the fisherman's life, and the life of the boy in the city; but the central thought in them all is the thought of the home.

After these lessons, the children should be taught to sing "Home, Sweet Home," and one stanza of the song has been inserted on page fifty, under the picture of the old homestead, in order to give them an opportunity to see in print the words which they are accustomed to recite, and to find some words which are already their familiar acquaintance. Later, this selection may be used as the nursery rhymes have been,

THE FIRST YEAR IN READING.   55

but it will be helpful even if it simply serves as an exercise in finding the familiar forms.

The wise teacher will make good use of the picture which represents the old home. — What could children do if they lived in a home like that? What could they play? What would they see? How is this home different from their home?

Many of the pictures in the book have been prepared, not simply to illustrate the lesson in hand, but with the thought of such study. If other pictures are not at hand, the teacher may turn from page to page in the book to find pictures that illustrate farm life, and life by the sea or in the woods.

XIV.

STUDY OF OCCUPATIONS.

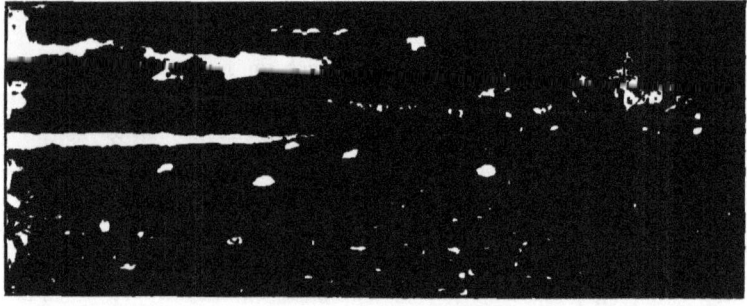

The hayfield and haymakers are introduced to the children on page fifty-one. The home, half hidden among the trees, is seen over the brow of the hill; they travel from the hill home to the hayfield, to watch the haymakers. Here is the first introduction in the book to the occupations of the men, about which they will learn much as they read. On another page, some suggestions are made in regard to the observation of the work and the workers in the neighborhood of the schools: the farmer, the blacksmith, the mason, the woodcutter, etc. This lesson upon the haymakers points in the same direction, and should be supplemented and extended after some observation of the materials and the occupations noted in the lesson. Later, the farmer will be studied in the same way; — likewise the miller, the churner, and the blacksmith. Every thoughtful observation of the outside life will reënforce the reading, and help the children to realize that books are written to teach them, and to help them to understand what they see. The stronger the relation of the child's experience to his text in reading, the more helpful will the other lessons become.

On page fifty-three, the children begin the reading of lessons upon the sun. They are glad in the sunshine, and they talk about the gifts of the sun; they know they are happier when it is sunny than when it is cloudy, dark, and dismal. Their smiles are like sunshine; they give thanks for the sunshine, and strive to be sunny and glad, to play that they are sunbeams. In this connection, a copy of Sir Joshua Reynolds' beautiful picture is introduced. The faces which are here pictured are so lovely that even the children realize how a child's face serves to make the world beautiful.

On page sixty, the children who have been reading of making sunshine have given them the song of the earth full of music, with its sunshine. This poem should be read to them until it is memorized. It is intended as a memory gem, to be taught in the ordinary way, and to help to emphasize the thought which the preceding lessons should have given. With singing birds and glad sunshine there should be happy children to make the world complete. The teacher, if she chooses, may use the exercise for word study, after the memorizing; but, if the lessons have been taught in the spirit which the subjects suggest, enough will have been gained if the poem is simply memorized.

Later in the year, the children may return to it and read it for themselves. It is introduced at this juncture because of its helpful meaning.

XV.

THE VOWELS.

On page sixty-four, the long sounds of the vowels are introduced. Hitherto, stress has been laid upon the short sounds simply because they occur more frequently in the early reading, and because the long sound introduces the difficult silent letter. Now the children have had sufficient experience to distinguish between the different sounds, and to name the long sound and conquer the difficulties involved in the use of silent letters in their phonic analysis. The device which has been used to help them memorize the vowels is very like that which was employed in the alphabetical word list. The initial letters of the names of five girls are the vowels in full. **A** for **Ada**, **E** for **Eva**, **I** for **Ida**, **O** for **Ora**, **U** for **Una**. The initial sound of these words is the long sound of the corresponding vowel. The illustrations which accompany the lesson are an attractive feature of the page. After reading this page, the pupils may include in their word study exercises in finding vowels, and in marking them as either long or short.

The exercise upon page sixty-seven suggests a form of word study for the children. Words which contain the same vowel sound are collected in the lists. The power to make these lists indicates some degree of comprehension of phonic analysis.

XVI.

GOOD LITERATURE.

On page sixty-eight, appears one of Robert Louis Stevenson's charming child poems. All children are merry at the thought of the good cow who gives them cream to eat with apple tart, but no child will dream how much he is getting when he memorizes the words of the poem. Here he begins to read for himself something which is included in good literature. A plea for such reading has been made elsewhere. Teachers are everywhere recognizing its value. The vocabulary of the Reader if carefully collated would serve to show that the hope of preparing the children to read good literature has governed the selections in the book, from beginning to end.

Nor will the vocabulary alone tell the story. The fashion of a sentence may be crude and heavy, even if the words are well chosen. But the graceful phrases of Stevenson's poems are not too difficult for children, and the simple sentences of the First Reader, or of the lesson upon the board, may be expressed in graceful fashion and poetical phrase, and still be entirely within the comprehension of the child. Upon page seventy-one, are written two sentences which all lovers of literature like to recall, and yet they are simple enough for the children's reading. In succeeding lessons, the brook appears and reappears, thus making ready for Tennyson's "Song of the Brook." It should be read to the children after these lessons have been read by them. It is to be hoped that the teacher who uses this book will read to the children from the best of books, and help them to realize that their mastery of the simple lessons is an open sesame to these golden fields.

XVII.

SCRIPT LESSONS.

The Script Lessons which are distributed through the book are intended to afford occupation for the study period. They are written with clear and graceful type, and place an excellent copy before the children. On page ninety-three, the charming verses of Mary Mapes Dodge are written in script. They are worthy of frequent copying.

Little Girl.
Good morrow, pretty Rosebush!
 I pray you tell me true.
To be as sweet as a red, red rose,
 What must a body do?

Rosebush.
To be as sweet as a red, red rose,
 A little girl like you,
Just grows, and grows, and grows, and grows,
 And that's what she must do.

MARY MAPES DODGE.

*Permission of the Century Co.
Publishers of "St. Nicholas."*

XVIII.

THE FABLE.

Fables and folk stories are always attractive to children. No other form of story is so popular. This has ever been the case, as the long life of the Fable testifies. Some of the best known fables have been put into simple language for the readers of this book, an attempt having been made to render them in conversational style, so that there may be variety in reading as well as interest in the story. The moral has been put in the form of a proverb when possible. In the fables, it has been thought well to sacrifice the teacher's ordinary standard of the vocabulary to the interest of the story and the style of expression. A number of new words appear in the fables. To omit them, or to substitute familiar and easy ones, would lower the standard of expression. It is believed that the children will find the fables worth mastering as they are written. Into these stories some expressions and phrases are introduced which purposely assume a figurative form. It is time for the children to begin such reading. The language of literature is different from the language of conversation, and will ever be. **The hare sped like the wind**, is more difficult to master than **The hare ran fast**, but it is worth all it costs.

The folk story of the "Mouse in the oven spinning blue wool" has ever been a favorite with children. The repetition is a delight to them. Here we make amends in full for the hard work in the fable; for the words of the mouse, in the story, are repeated over and over again. What is the secret of the children's delight in this story? The teacher who answers this question will know how to choose reading for her pupils.

XIX.

THE MISSION OF THE PICTURE.

In preparing this series of books, no effort has been spared to secure reproductions of the best pictures that children like; yet it may happen that so great emphasis is laid upon the reading of the text that the mission of the picture will be forgotten. Within the First Reader are included Millet's "Churner," and "Feeding the Birds," Meyer von Bremen's "Little Nurse," and Sir Joshua Reynolds' "Angels' Heads." The children should talk about the pictures, tell what they see in them and how they like them, recur to them again and again as they turn the pages of the book, the teacher never passing them without some comment upon their beauty.

Upon page 105, the subject of the lesson is the Mother, whom the children love better than any one else.

She is the dearest mother in the world.
Her smile is like the sunshine.
Her voice is as sweet as a song.
She is busy from morning till night.
It is mother who makes our dresses.
It is mother who gets our dinner.
It is mother who tells us pretty stories.
It is mother who sings us pretty songs.
It is mother who loves us.
And we love her with all our hearts.

If the teacher succeeds in making the children feel as they ought to feel when they read this lesson, and when they repeat [1] "Hundreds of stars in the pretty sky,"—they will be quite ready to interpret the picture of the artist. The three children sit in the open door of the cottage; the mother with the bowl in her lap leans forward to feed her children with the wooden spoon. How intent they are, as they eagerly wait for the coming food! The little one in the middle leans forward for her portion; the others await their turn in eager confidence. How good the mother is, and how the children love her! How she loves the children! Why does the artist call the picture "Feeding the Birds"? The child who can read the lesson can read the picture.

Just as this picture shows mother life, the "Churner" represents the sturdy homeliness of the worker, at her common task. The child who reads the lesson can thank Elsie for making the yellow butter. He begins to think of the many hands that are working for him, and to look upon the honest laborer with honest respect. Some such feeling the study of the picture will add to his lesson; and if the teacher stops to tell the children of the artist's choice of subject and his reason for so choosing, their thoughts will recur to the lesson in days to come, and the picture will grow in meaning as the children grow in experience. Do not omit the study of the picture.

[1] See page 105, First Reader.

Part III.

LANGUAGE LESSONS AS AN AID TO READING.

Part III.
CHAPTER IV.

LANGUAGE LESSONS AS AN AID TO READING.

STUDY OF THE MEANING OF WORDS.

IN the preceding chapters, reference has been made to the fact that the child's experience largely determines his interpretation of the reading lesson. All teachers will readily recall incidents in their own class-work which will illustrate this truth. The child who has never seen the ocean, whose life, perhaps, has been spent in the mountains, will find it difficult to picture the scenes which are described in the story of "The Leak in the Dike." The mountain walls to which he has been accustomed are very different from the low level fields which the little Dutch boy has known. The wideness of the sea, its tides, its mighty strength, are notions which may be entirely strange to him. So, also, any child who lives in an inland village or town, needs some helper to make plain to him the poems and stories which describe the life of the sea. "The Wreck of the Hesperus" is written in a foreign tongue to him whose imagination has never depicted the raging waves, the cruel rocks, the pebbly beach, the bitter storm, and the shattered ship. As we read the poem, every word is filled with meaning because our associations have enriched our lives with varied experiences. We have walked on the beach, have climbed over the rocks, have watched the vessel slowly sinking from sight below the distant horizon, have waited for the steady advance of the incoming tide, and heard the restless waters beating upon the steadfast rocks. We have seen the stately vessels riding upon the still waters of the bay, or tossing upon the waves of the outer ocean. We have talked with the sailors, and know something of their sturdy lives, and the fearful dangers to which they are exposed. We know boys and girls who have sailed with their fathers on long voyages. All this knowledge illuminates the poem, and fills it with meaning for us. Bereft of this experience, we should fail to catch the beauty of the poet's description or to read his meaning in the familiar lines. It requires some effort of the imagination to enable us to conceive how little Emerson's snowstorm would say to us if our eyes had never beheld the gathering storm, "announced by all the trumpets of the sky." Bryant's "Fringed Gentian" is written for those whose eyes have delighted in the exquisite beauty of the autumn blossom. "The Death of the Flowers" must be interpreted by him who knows the windflower and the violet, the aster and the golden rod. The perfect picture of June, in Lowell's "Vision of Sir Launfal," is visible only to him whose eyes have seen the buttercup catching "the sun in its chalice" and whose ears have been attuned to the music of the bird whose "illumined being" overruns "with the deluge of summer it receives."

The experience of the children is akin to our own. Whatever they read is interpreted by what they have seen and heard and felt. Many a word which seems to us so simple and common that we pass it unchallenged in our teaching, stands apart from all experience in the children's lives, calls up no notions in their minds, fails altogether to contribute to the meaning of the story which they are reading. However simple the lesson may be, the word which represents no idea to the child, is a stumbling-block and hinders the thought getting. It is utterly idle to insist upon the mere repetition of the word which serves in no degree to enlighten the child. The teacher who attempts to explain its meaning may contribute little to his enlightenment. The explanation is often given in terms which are quite as unintelligible as the original word. One bit of experience is worth a thousand explanations. A summer day in the country does more to interpret Lowell's picture of the day in June than would a hundred folios on the subject if the reader had never seen the fields and the flowers. Just so, the child who is to read about the chicken, the cow, the tortoise, the oak, the violet, the frost, must gain his insight through sight. Lessons which supply the experience to those who have never had it, or which recall the forgotten experience so that it illumines the text, are legitimate reading lessons. Indeed, they are indispensable.

It is therefore the duty of the teacher to discover in what lines the child is ignorant, and to help him to increase his knowledge therein. This increase must come through actual seeing and doing on his part, as has been said. Observation lessons whose object is to lead the children to new knowledge, are not only useful in developing facility in expression and keenness in observing, but also in preparing the pupils to read the pages in which these objects are described. If the object which figures in the lesson is unattainable as well as unknown, the picture may suffice. If this is not to be secured, the teacher's explanation may be made to suffice — as a last resort.

It should not be forgotten, however, that the child's doing is much more potent than the teacher's telling — nor that the description which seems clear to the teacher may be obscure to the child. "What are the ornaments in the room?" questioned a pupil just learning the language. "Oh, the knickknacks," replied the teacher. The pupil was quite as much in the dark as before his question. The explanation must be couched in terms of the learner's experience, and must take full account of his limitations. If this simple principle were always followed, much of the misdirected energy and the consequent tedium of the schoolroom would be spared.

Applying this principle to the work with the little children, we shall conclude that lessons on things must contribute to the power to interpret the words which represent thought and experience. Language lessons, observation lessons, field lessons, etc. will become familiar features in the series of lessons which aim to teach children to read.

In the primary Readers which this manual accompanies, the objects described are selected with reference to the interests of ordinary children, as they have been carefully studied. The further purpose has been to interest children in their environment, in nature and human nature. A running glance will discover the lines which have been chosen, and the kind of contributing lessons which are desirable. The following lists name forms of animal and plant life, natural forces, and minerals, to which reference is made in the primary Readers, with allusions to the common occupations of men.

ANIMALS.

FIRST READER.

dog	robin	ox	tortoise
cow	bluebird	lamb	fish
cat	oriole	sheep	worms
mouse	eggs	wool	shells
hen	goat	squirrel	bee
chickens	horse	fox	butterfly

SECOND READER.

goose	sparrows	stag	trout
turkey	blue jay	hound	quail
crow	kid	rabbit	flies
eagle	wolf	donkey	ant
crane	bear	frog	grasshopper
dove	lion	turtle	sponges

THIRD READER.

pigeons	crow	curlew	salmon
woodpecker	raven	sandpiper	beetle
swallows	wren	toads	spaniel
blackbird	duck	vipers	hedgehog

PLANT LIFE.

FIRST READER.

tree	pine	windflower	corn
orchard	oak	violet	tassel
apples	acorn	snowdrop	ears
branches	pussy willow	asters	husks
roots	lily	dandelion	wheat
maple	rose	clover	vine

SECOND READER.

grapes	bramble	beans	hawthorn
blueberries	weeds	peas	cedar
fig	nuts	lettuce	daisies
raisins	peanuts	radishes	columbine
chestnut	hazel	fir tree	elder-bloom

THIRD READER.

olive trees	marigolds	morning-glories	flax
birch	tulips	anemone	spices
tamarack	peonies	fern	cucumber
holly	poppy	beeches	onions
sycamore	hyacinth	burdock	potatoes

OCCUPATIONS.

FIRST READER.

farming churning spinning blacksmith

SECOND READER.

fishing threshing fuller author
weaving shearing soldier artist
mowing sexton statesman charcoal-burner

THIRD READER.

woodman gleaner engineer sailor
ditcher tailor miller merchant

NATURAL PHENOMENA.

FIRST READER.

sun rainbow rain wind
sky stars snow northwind
clouds showers dewdrops spring

SECOND READER.

moon	hail	Jack Frost	mountain
dawn	icicles	summer	hill
night	lake	winter	valley

reflection in the water

THIRD READER.

storm   echo   freshet   fountain

MINERALS.

gold   pearls   coal   salt   diamonds

It is not expected that the teacher's plan will include an exhaustive study of all the facts and objects suggested. But it is absolutely necessary that the children should have some clear and general notion of the meaning of the words used, so that their reading will be intelligent, the words truly representing ideas to their minds. The accompanying lessons are intended to suggest and illustrate types of lessons which should accompany lessons in reading, whenever the pupil's knowledge is so limited as to hinder the process of thought getting. It should not be forgotten that the teacher must be the best judge as to the best selection of subjects for her own class. Further, the teacher will recognize that any of these lessons may serve to reënforce her teaching in language, drawing, or nature study, as well as reading.

Part IV.

ILLUSTRATIVE LESSONS.

OBSERVATION, LANGUAGE, AND PREPARATION FOR READING.

Part IV.

CHAPTER V.

I.

LESSON UPON THE COW.

TO precede or accompany Reading Lessons which refer to the cow.
(*in lowest grades*)

I. Find out what the children know about the cow.

Every new lesson should be built upon, and fastened to, the child's past experience. If the children have no knowledge of cows, we must introduce the subject accordingly. If they have always known them, the lesson will be merely a review, because the foundation will have been prepared. If the children live in the country and know the common animals, proceed at once to definite questions which will arrange their knowledge and help them to express it.

Where have you seen cows? What do you know about them, — their size, color, the head, ears, legs, feet, tail?

How large are they, as compared with the horse, dog, cat?

Compare the covering with that of the horse, dog, cat. Compare the parts with the corresponding parts of those animals.

Describe the horns. Why do cows have horns? What use do they make of them?

Describe the ears. Where are they? Does the cow move them? (The ears of the dog, cat, cow, horse are movable; ours are not. Why?)

Compare the cow's nose and mouth with those of the cat or the horse.

Does any one know anything about the cow's teeth? What does she eat? What kind of teeth does she need?

Tell the children about the chewing of the cud.

Of what use to the cow is the long tail with its brush at the end? Who has seen her use it? Would a short tail serve as well?

Who knows anything about the cow's foot? Who can draw a picture of the cow's footprint?

Of what use are cows to us? What does the cow give to us?

How should cows be cared for? What kind of stall, what kind of bed, what food, water, pasture, should they have? Describe a pasture you would like if you were a cow.

How ought we to treat animals? Is it right to forget their wants when we have the care of them?

Every lesson upon animals should help the children to realize more fully their obligation to properly care for them. Sympathy for animal life ought to be developed through the reading and language lessons. Interest in animal life is always present in children. The questions above suggested cannot be answered at once, by any ordinary class of children. Many who are familiar with cows in general will be unable to answer the definite questions. The questions will lead them to a more careful observation, after which they can report in another lesson. Sometimes the questions may be distributed, different groups of children being held responsible for the answers to certain ones.

II. Direct outside observation in order to get new knowledge.

It is entirely feasible, in many schoolrooms, to make the cow the subject of a field lesson. The children may be taken, in groups, to a farmyard, a pasture, or a stable, where a cow may be observed and studied. Such lessons have ceased to be formidable, since they have become so common. The need of such visits is revealed by the children's vague answers. Nothing but definite observation of the real thing will open their eyes, and make the words in their lesson full of meaning.

There are many city children who have never seen a cow. If it is impossible to show them a real cow, excellent pictures should be substituted. Many of the questions suggested could be answered by pictures. It must be remembered, however, that the picture tells to us, who have seen the real thing, much more than it tells to a child, who has never had that experience. It is not strange that a child who has never seen a real cow should imagine that animal to be six inches long, the size of the cow which he has known from pictures in the lesson. Emphasize the fact of the size. Allude to the picture as a picture only. Have the children show by their hands how high a cow would be, how long, how wide its head, etc. By such means, help to vivify the mental picture which is suggested to the child by the lesson. If the pictures are the only avenues through which the children learn about the cow, do not attempt to give as much information as would naturally be associated with the real observation lesson. Remember that the amount of knowledge which the child gains is not proportioned to the number of facts enumerated by the teacher. He will intelligently appropriate those which his observation and thought have helped him to understand. As has been said before, this truth determines the value of the reading lesson to the child, and necessitates the associated lessons which supplement his experience and enable him to bring to the lesson a mind furnished with appropriate ideas.

III. Tell the children simple facts which they cannot find out for themselves.

There are many facts associated with the cow which the children can know only through others: the use of the horns, of the bones, the hair, etc.; the manufactures; the reason for the cud-chewing; — the making of butter and cheese. The writer has known classrooms in which milk was skimmed, the cream churned into butter, and the butter eaten by the children. The quantity, of course, was small, but the process was very real and very interesting. This happened recently in a kindergarten in the city. There were only three children in the class who had ever seen a cow. It is hardly necessary to say that the lesson followed a visit to that animal.

IV. Reënforce the lessons by stories.

Stories about cows, or descriptions of certain animals, perhaps the pets which we have known, will add interest to the lessons.

V. Collect pictures of cows, for comparison and description.

In almost any district the children will be able to help in making collections of pictures which illustrate the language and reading lesson. These pictures can be obtained from newspapers, magazines, advertisements, and various other sources. Every child who helps to swell the collection will feel an added interest in it. The collection will be valuable in proportion as it is carefully arranged and thoughtfully used by the teacher. If the cards are neatly mounted upon separate sheets which contain the name of the contributor, and distributed amongst the children for observation and comparison, it will prove really helpful. Through the comparison of the different pictures, many facts will be developed, suggested by the children's comments or questions. Such teaching will be sure to fit the needs of the children. These suggestions will be modified and arranged by any teacher who desires to use them. They may help to point the way for those who are not entirely familiar with this phase of their work.

II.

LESSON UPON THE OAK.

As in the lesson upon the cow, the teacher's first object should be to discover what the children already know. Nearly all children, even those living in cities or towns, have some opportunity to see and study trees, and their attention should be carefully directed to those about them.

Have you ever seen an oak tree? Where was it growing? How tall was it? (Compare with a man, a horse, a house; with other trees.)

What do you remember about the size of its trunk? About the bark, about the leaves, about the fruit?

Bring to the class acorns, leaves, or, in blossom time, bring blossoms.

What is the use of the blossom, the leaf, the acorn?

Draw them.

Plant an acorn and see what comes of it.

(Patient and continued observation.)

Of what use is the oak tree to us? (Do not forget that beauty as well as manufacturing is to be considered.)

Name articles made of oak.

Bring specimens of the wood.
The older pupils can draw the tree.
Tell the children about the Charter Oak.
Take them, if possible, to a field, or wood or park or street where they can see an oak growing.
Refer to the lesson some weeks afterwards, in order to lead to continued observation of the tree in different stages.
Do not feel that it is necessary to do all which the lesson suggests with every class, but be sure that the children have some actual knowledge of an actual oak tree.

III.

LESSONS UPON OCCUPATIONS.

Frequent reference is made, in all literature, to the occupations of men. Even if this were not the case, a knowledge of these occupations is necessary to even a fair education. Every child should have some intelligent knowledge of the work of the farmer, the miller, the carpenter, the bricklayer, the engineer, the miner, the merchant. But, be this as it may, the pages of the school Reader, will demand some knowledge of the every day occupations of men.

Children are naturally interested in the occupations of their neighbors. They like to see things made. They like to know why certain effects come from certain causes. Nothing could be more fruitful than a visit to a blacksmith shop, a new house that is being built, a sewer that is being dug, a cellar that is being laid; to a ropewalk, to a mine, to a quarry, where real men are engaged in real work. The natural interest of children in these subjects is evidenced by their desire to "play" the miller, the farmer, the driver, the boatman, etc. We do well when we build upon this natural interest. "The Village Blacksmith" is a familiar poem based upon a common experience. As has been said, the children who know something about the work of the blacksmith will enjoy and understand the poem as no others can. Ask them to go to a blacksmith and then to report; or go with a class of children, and help them to observe and question. The blacksmith will be courteous and generous if he is courteously requested to give his aid to the children. Prepare them for the lesson by a preliminary talk about the blacksmith, his work, the need of his work; his tools, the material with which he works, the sources from which iron is obtained, the process by which steel is made. Having prepared the children to observe, assign questions or topics upon which they are to report: the anvil, the forge, the sledge, the bellows, the horseshoe, etc. Upon their return from the visit, allow the different pupils to tell what they have seen. After the general conversation, insist upon an orderly description.

Kindred lessons may be given upon the other occupations suggested. In many cases stories can be told or read, which will reënforce the observation. It must not be forgotten that one result of the lessons should be a sincere respect for honest toil, and a pride in the ability to do honest work well. It is hardly necessary to say that the visit to the blacksmith's shop will reënforce the reading, and that a study of Longfellow's poem will, in turn, make the visit more valuable. The language lesson will help the reading lesson because it adds interest; it will also help the lesson as literature, because it gives fuller power of interpretation and corresponding appreciation of the poem. All these lessons will be made more valuable by the use of collections of pictures.

RAIN.

FOR SECOND GRADE.

Observation during a rain.
What is rain?
Where does it come from?

How did it get there?
Experiment later, if the children become interested in the question. Do not answer it for them now. Let them question and think.
Upon which windows does it fall?
Why not upon the opposite windows?
Where does it go?
What good will it do?
Think what the rain does for the trees. How do you know?
What does it do for the birds? How do you know?
What does it do for the flowers? How do you know?
What does it do for you?
If no rain were to fall for three months, what would happen to the flowers, to the grass, to the gardens, to the brooks?
Would it make any difference to you?
Experiment: —
Breathe upon the cold glass. Show condensed vapor.
Boil water: collect vapor on cold surface.
Recall vapor on windows.
Recall clothes drying.
Recall windows on washing day.
Explain how fine particles of water are carried through the air, unite so as to be seen when cold, — in breath, on windows, in clouds, in fog.
Explain how rainfall is caused.
Read "Children of the Clouds."
Memorize "Is it Raining, Little Flower?"
Read to the children " A Rainy Day " (*Longfellow*).
Tell the story of the drop of water in its journey from ocean to ocean again.
Ask them to reproduce the story.

IV.

LESSONS ON BIRD LIFE.

The study of birds has become so common a feature of school work, that suggestions on the subject may be trite and superfluous. For those teachers who have not yet attempted such study, the following practical suggestions may be helpful.

All children are interested in animal life, but few city children have more than a vague notion of the habits and characteristics of the animals of which they read. Not long ago the writer chanced to hear a class of primary children reading about the hen. The exercise was hesitating, the reading dubious. Upon questioning, it was found that but three children in the class had ever seen a live hen, and in two of these cases the hen was "nailed up in a box in the market." One child only had seen a hen walking about, and that was in "Tim Jones's alley." Obviously the sentences which had seemed so luminous to the teacher were dark to the children.

Such experiences are not confined to city children. Wide experience has discovered many a country child whose eyes have never been truly opened to the life about him. It is safe to assume that any class of little children will profit by any lesson which increases their interest in the bird world, and opens their eyes to see new beauties and their minds to receive new pictures, and which incidentally explains the pages that otherwise are meaningless.

For such preliminary study, the best beginning is the observation of some caged bird, which can be kept within reach for awhile. A canary, a parrot, a dove, a hen, a duck, will behave well in the schoolroom, may be cared for by the pupils, and studied for several days, and will serve as a center from which new investigations may radiate, or as a type to which all new bird-knowledge may be referred. The canary or parrot can be brought in its own house. For the others a dwelling place may be extemporized. A box frame may be built, open on all sides, and covered with coarse wire netting, or, better, with fencing. Or the one side may be removed from a wooden box of suitable size, and netting be substituted for it. The children should be able to watch the bird as it eats, drinks, walks or flies about, and should be allowed at first to observe without the restriction of question or recitation.

The conversation of the pupils, their exclamations and questions, will reveal the best line of approach to the subject. It will be found that their chief interest centers in the actions of the bird. "See him eat!" "How fast he turns the seed!" "See the shells fly!" "How he spatters the water!" "Oh, he's washing himself!" Such are the free comments of the children.

Let these determine the first lesson.

You have been watching the canary, what have you seen him do? What can he do that you do? What can he do that you cannot do?

These questions cannot be answered without actual knowledge. If the replies are written upon the board, it will be discovered that the children have added definitely to their store of knowledge, and likewise to their vocabulary.

Another conversation may compare the cat and the canary, the cow and the canary, or (a very different exercise) may note the resemblances and differences between the canary and other birds with which the children are somewhat familiar. This comparison leads to observation of the structure, to naming and describing the parts of the canary.

"The canary can fly because he has wings. We have no wings but we have arms. The cat has no wings but she has two fore-legs." So the comparison proceeds to head, eyes, bill, feet, until the children are ready to describe the bird in clear and appropriate language.

Another talk compares the habits of the bird with those of the cat and dog, and leads to descriptions of the nests, the eggs, the home habits of the bird with the rearing of the young. The lessons prepare for the reading, to be sure, but this value is incidental only, as compared with the evident interest and the growing power of the children in thinking, seeing, and saying.

It would be interesting to keep a record of the words used, or needed, by the children in such lessons, to collect them afterwards, and to discover what proportion of the list of words is included in the ordinary stock vocabulary of elementary readers. Such a study would reveal to any intelligent teacher the close relation between experience and reading, and would fully justify the plan of work outlined in these pages.

It may be well to add in passing that such a series of lessons serves as a basis to which all related lessons may be referred. When the children read about the oriole or the robin, he is compared with the canary, and the old lesson explains and reënforces the new. The value of such lessons depends upon the teacher's recognition of this relation. The children need not know the skeleton of her plan, but she must know the end from the beginning.

V.

STUDY OF "THE BUILDERS." — LONGFELLOW.

Preparation for the Poem.

If the readers are young children, it would be well to prepare for the reading of the poem by a lesson upon the material building. It is possible that the carpenters and masons are already at work in the immediate neighborhood of the schoolhouse. The children have been interested in watching the digging of the cellar, the laying of the foundation stone, the fixing of the frame in position, the laying of the walls. A little questioning and observation will lead them to see how necessary it is to the strength of the building that every part be well shaped and firmly placed. There may be unfortunate examples in their neighborhood which show the folly of dishonest building. They may easily be led to realize what harm may result from slighting any piece of work, or falsely covering any weakness. Anecdotes are abundant to illustrate this: the bridge which gives way beneath the weight of the passing train, carrying hundreds to death; the dam which has weak timber, yielding to the pressure of the freshet; the elevator which falls with its precious load. These point to building which was insecure and treacherous. For the other side of the picture, we turn to the old cathedrals, showing the children the beautiful spires, the exquisite carving, and telling them how they have endured through the ages because their builders did honest work.

Such a lesson prepares for the interpretation of the poem, which turns our thought to the building which we are shaping with our to-days and yesterdays. The lessons of the unstable wall, the falling bridge, as well as the grace and strength of the cathedral, serve now as a parallel for the poet's teaching, and the inevitable result to others is seen as well as felt when we read of the "broken stairways, where the feet stumble as they seek to climb." After such lessons, every line is filled with meaning as the children read and re-read the inspiring poem. Then it is time to memorize every line, but especially the two stanzas, —

> "In the elder days of art,
> Builders wrought with greatest care
> Each minute and unseen part;
> For the gods see everywhere.
>
> "Let us do our work as well,
> Both the unseen and the seen:
> Make the house, where gods may dwell,
> Beautiful, entire, and clean."

It is not necessary to preach while teaching this poem. The lesson impresses itself upon the children if they are rightly prepared for it. They will make their own application, but we should not forget that a valuable lesson like this is not measured by ease in recitation or accuracy in reading. If, in the days to come, the memory of the poet's words shall give strength in the hour of temptation, or incite to honest work when the hand inclines to careless shirking, the lesson will have counted for good. In selecting the poems for our children, and in directing their reading, such hope should guide our choice. The words of the poem or the story will recur again and again when the memory of the schoolroom has faded. We should be assured that the minds of our pupils are furnished with thoughts worth remembering. "Whatsoever things are lovely, whatsoever things are pure, whatsoever things are of good report, if there be any virtue, and if there be any praise, think on these things."

VI.

STUDY OF A POEM.

Illustrative Lesson.

LITTLE BELL.

Piped the blackbird on the beechwood spray,
"Pretty maid, slow wandering this way,
    What's your name?" quoth he, —
"What's your name? Oh, stop, and straight unfold,
Pretty maid, with showery curls of gold!"
    "Little Bell," said she.

Little Bell sat down beneath the rocks,
Tossed aside her gleaming golden locks.

"Bonny bird," quoth she,
"Sing me your best song, before I go."
"Here's the very finest song I know,
    Little Bell," said he.

And the blackbird piped; you never heard
Half so gay a song from any bird, —
    Full of quips and wiles,
Now so round and rich, now soft and slow,
    Dimpled o'er with smiles.

And the while the bonny bird did pour
His full heart out freely, o'er and o'er,
    'Neath the morning skies,
In the little childish heart below
All the sweetness seemed to grow and grow,
And shine forth in happy overflow
    From the blue, bright eyes.

Down the dell she tripped, and through the glade
Peeped the squirrel from the hazel shade,
    And from out the tree
Swung, and leaped, and frolicked, void of fear,
While bold blackbird piped, that all might hear,
    "Little Bell!" piped he.

Little Bell sat down amid the fern:
"Squirrel, squirrel, to your task return;
    Bring me nuts," quoth she.

Up, away, the frisky squirrel hies, —
Golden wood lights glancing in his eyes, —
    And adown the tree
Great ripe nuts, kissed brown by July sun,
In the little lap dropped, one by one.
Hark! how blackbird pipes to see the fun!
    "Happy Bell!" pipes he.

Little Bell looked up and down the glade:
"Squirrel, squirrel, if you 're not afraid,
    Come and share with me!"
Down came squirrel, eager for his fare, —
Down came bonny blackbird, I declare!
Little Bell gave each his honest share;
    Ah, the merry three!

And the while these frolic playmates twain
Piped and frisked from bough to bough again,
    'Neath the morning skies,
In the little childish heart below
All the sweetness seemed to grow and grow,
And shine out in happy overflow
    From her blue, bright eyes.

By her snow-white cot, at close of day,
Knelt sweet Bell, with folded palms, to pray:
    Very calm and clear
Rose the praying voice, to where, unseen,
In blue heaven, an angel shape serene
    Paused awhile to hear.

"What good child is this," the angel said,
"That, with happy heart, beside her bed
 Prays so lovingly?"
Low and soft, — oh! very low and soft,
Crooned the blackbird in the orchard croft,
 "Bell, dear Bell!" crooned he.

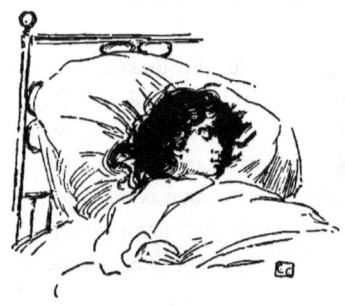

"Whom God's creatures love," the angel fair
Murmured, "God doth bless with angels' care;
 Child, thy bed shall be
Folded safe from harm. Love, deep and kind,
Shall watch around, and leave good gifts behind,
 Little Bell, for thee."

THOMAS WESTWOOD.

The poem selected for this lesson is suitable for use in third, fourth, or fifth grades, although even younger children enjoy hearing it read. Such children would, however, find difficulty in a detailed study, such as is suggested in this exercise. The poem may be used simply as a reading lesson, or it may be read, studied, and memorized by the pupils as a language exercise. The various advantages of the study are indicated in the following suggestions, which are intended to indicate merely some of the different modes of treatment which may be attempted in language teaching.

The Thought in the Poem.

As in all lessons, the children should read the entire poem or hear it read before any detailed study is attempted. This is done in order that the poem may be presented to them as a whole, giving its thought or telling its message. After such reading, every stanza and every word will assume its rightful place in the description of the story. Otherwise, given separately, the words lose the meaning which they are intended to convey. A poem, like a picture, should be presented as a whole, and never dissected, in the first lesson.

It is wise, sometimes, to read and to re-read without note or comment; then to lay aside the book and leave the children to recall the story, and to accustom themselves to its pictures. At the next lesson, the teacher may question, — following out any of the suggested lines of work.

The important motive is to get the message which the author intended to give us in the poem. Everything else must be subordinate to this purpose. Any supplementary teaching which draws the attention away from the poem, creating a separate center of interest, is in excess. All illustration and explanation should be intended simply to throw light upon the poem, making the pictures more vivid and the message more plain.

The thought in this poem is very evident, even to the children. In the first stanza the blackbird on the beechwood spray introduces us to the pretty maid, slow wandering his way. She is little Bell. Sitting down beneath the rocks, she asks the blackbird for his best song. The bonny bird pours his full heart out freely, while in the little childish heart below, all the sweetness seems to grow and grow, and shine forth in happy overflow from the blue, bright eyes. The squirrel swings and leaps and frolics in the glade, and at the child's bidding drops down great ripe nuts into her lap. The blackbird pipes to see the fun. The child shares her treasures with the squirrel and the bird, and again the poet tells us

> "In the little childish heart below
> All the sweetness seemed to grow and grow,
> And shine out in happy overflow
> From her blue, bright eyes."

When, at close of day, the child kneels to pray beside her snow-white cot, an angel pauses to hear, and asks what good child prays so lovingly beside her bed. The blackbird answers from the orchard croft, "Bell, dear Bell!" "Whom God's creatures love, God doth bless with angels' care," the angel murmured.

> "Child, thy bed shall be
> Folded safe from harm. Love, deep and kind,
> Shall watch around, and leave good gifts behind,
> Little Bell, for thee."

Even the little children sense the meaning of the poem. They have already learned that love wins love, and makes friends, and they feel it to be both natural and just that the loving little Bell shall be shielded from all harm, and sheltered by loving thought. The older children may be reminded of Sidney Lanier's poem, "How Love Sought for Hell," — failing to find it because wherever his presence came there were kindness and light. The little ones are reminded that the mirror gives back smile for smile, and frown for frown. It is hardly necessary to point the moral and adorn the tale. The poet has repeated in the selfsame words the lines which show how the child grew in sweetness as she played so lovingly with her woodland friends. For many classes it would be enough to talk of the poem until the children were possessed of this thought, or rather this feeling, and then leave it to do its own work. In this case, however, the poem serves as a text for the lesson, and we shall consider other phases.

PREPARATION FOR THE READING.
The Pictures in the Poem.

The poem takes us at once to the woods where the blackbird pipes on the beechwood spray. We see the rocks, the dell, the glade, the trees, the hazel shade, and are made acquainted with the blackbird and the squirrel. Plainly, the setting of the poem is clearest to those children who themselves have played in the woods; who have heard the blackbird sing, and have seen the squirrel leap from bough to bough. The beechwood spray, the hazel shade, the dell, the glade, the fern, are already familiar to such children, and need no lesson to introduce them. But if the tenement house, the narrow alley, the brick walls and the noisy street have been the familiar surroundings of the children, and if the country seems as far away to them as Paradise, the poem is written in a foreign tongue. With such children, other lessons are necessary before any such selection is read or memorized. These lessons may not be given at the time of the reading; far better not: but they should precede the reading in the teacher's plan, and the young reader should enter upon this lesson equipped with some knowledge of the bird, the squirrel, and the woods. In another chapter, something has been said of the necessity of such teaching, and of the way in which such lessons may be conducted. The suggestion is made here simply to emphasize this truth, — that observation of nature is essential to the interpretation of literature.

The Study of the Vocabulary of the Poem.

Although the pupils may be prepared by their out-of-door experience to understand the poem, nevertheless they will be met by a new difficulty in the reading. The language of literature differs from that to which they have been accustomed in conversation. The tendency of our school readers and children's books is often to remove such difficulties from the path of the children. The lessons are expressed in words already familiar to them, and in colloquial forms. While this practice renders the first lessons in reading easy, it makes the entrance to literature difficult. Many expressions are entirely foreign to the child's ear, and therefore unintelligible, even when the story is attractive. The poem which we are using for illustration contains many words and phrases which the children have not met in their ordinary reading. These must be explained and their meaning made familiar to the children. "'What's your name?' *quoth* he;" "stop, and *straight unfold;*" "*showery* curls of gold;" "*gleaming* golden locks;" "*bonny* bird;" "blackbird *piped;*" "dell;" "glade;" "hazel shade;" "*void* of fear;" "hies;" "golden wood lights;" "*adown* the tree;" "playmates twain;" "an angel shape;" "*crooned* the blackbird in the orchard croft," are some of these.

It may not be necessary nor wise in most classes to study all these expressions minutely, but they should become plain to the children so that they may plainly speak the message of the poem, and present no difficulty if met elsewhere. So with the figurative expressions: "The bird did pour his full heart out freely;" "the sweetness did shine forth in happy overflow;" "Thy bed shall be folded safe from harm;" "stop, and straight unfold."

There is no reason why the young readers should not come to realize the picture in these figurative expressions, to compare their several words with the figure which the poet has used, and to begin to sense the difference between plain, straightforward speech and the pictured verses of the poet. Such study, however simple, will help the children to some appreciation of the beauty of expression, which is one charm of literature.

From what has been said, it will be rightly judged that the poem affords a basis of several lessons, all of value in different directions. It may not be wise to make a detailed and careful study of every poem which is read or memorized by the children, but some teaching in the lines suggested is indispensable to intelligent reading on the part of the children. The phrases which are so familiar to us often suggest very curious ideas to the children. Their peculiar interpretation is shown when they draw pictures to represent the scenes of a poem or story. In a certain school, the teacher read a story to the children containing the expression, "his mother gave him leave to go." The child drew the mother in the act of presenting a leaf to the boy. "Fret-work," said the boy who read "Sir Launfal" for the first time, "Fret-work is work that makes you fret;" while the child who drew the picture of the hare and the tortoise represented a turtle and a boy with bushy hair. Reference has been made elsewhere to the kid on the roof of the house which was pictured as a little boy, and the writer remembers the pictures which were drawn by children in illustration of the above poem, representing the angels with webbed feet.[1] These items are intended simply to suggest that the child's crude notion is often very different from the meaning which the word or phrase conveys to us. Detailed study often reveals his error to us, if we bend a listening ear to his question or comment. We should be grateful for the frank question or the crude remark which betrays the child's mistake, and should be careful to secure such confidence and

---

[1] The illustrative lessons in this chapter are taken from "Reading: How to Teach it," a complete manual prepared by Miss Arnold and published by this house.

freedom in our classes as will enable us to discover what the children are really thinking.

After the reading and discussion of the poem, the children may memorize it. At this juncture, it is wise for the teacher to read it to the children again and again, in order that they may get some notion of the proper reading. This will not be necessary in all classes, but where the children are accustomed to dull or monotonous reading, some outside standard is necessary. The children's recitation will incline to adopt the virtues of the teacher's reading. Let us not forget that the faults will be imitated, too.

If after such study and such memorizing, the words of the poem appear now and then in the children's conversation or writing, let us rejoice, for this means not simply that new words have been added to the vocabulary, but that the child has a new conception of the beauty of thought as well as of speech.

www.ingramcontent.com/pod-product-compliance
Lightning Source LLC
Chambersburg PA
CBHW032239080426
42735CB00008B/925